START-A-CRAFT

Puppets

Get started in a new craft with easy-to-follow

projects for beginners

DEBORAH SCHNEEBELI-MORRELL

THE
APPLE
PRESS

A QUINTET BOOK

Published by The Apple Press
6 Blundell Street.
London N7 9BH

ISBN 1—85076—496—4

This book was designed and produced by
Quintet Publishing Limited
6 Blundell Street
London N7 9BH

Creative Director: Richard Dewing
Designer: James Lawrence
Project Editor: Stefanie Foster
Photographer: Heini Schneebeli

DEDICATION
For my father David
D.S.M.

Typeset in Great Britain by
Central Southern Typesetters, Eastbourne
Manufactured in Hong Kong by
Regent Publishing Services Limited
Printed in China

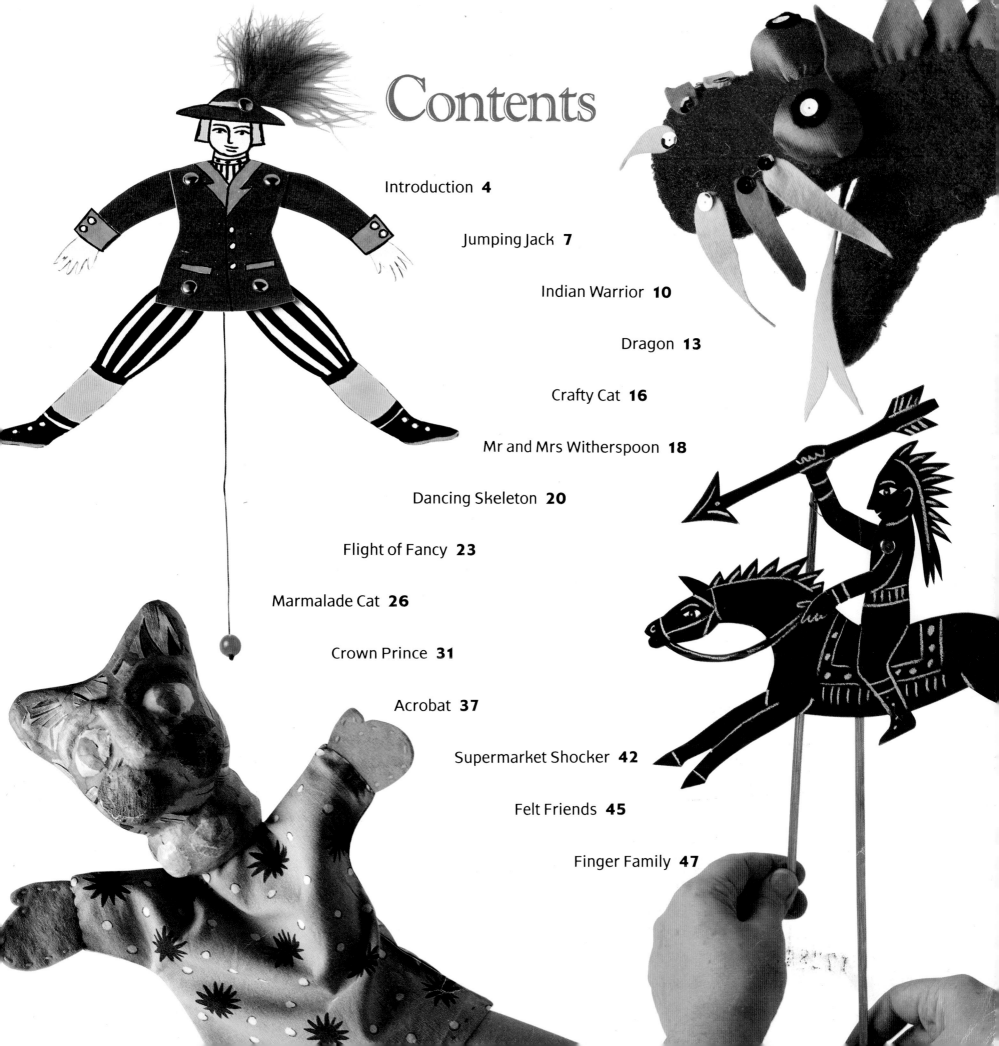

Contents

Introduction

• • •

Puppetry holds a fascination for adults and children alike, and this universal appeal is rooted in the ancient history and traditions of many cultures.

History and traditions

The oldest form of theatre in the world, it is widely believed that the origins of puppetry were in the far east. In both India and China puppets were used to recount legends and folk tales, to dramatise religious and moral teachings and it was a popular art both in the street and the Palace.

Most famous, perhaps, of the eastern puppets are the Waylang Purwa Shadow Puppets of Indonesia, made from beautifully painted and gilded oiled parchment. These were animated in front of a light thus casting shadows on a translucent screen, depicting stories of Gods, Demons and Heroes. The Egyptian, Greek and Roman cultures, too, all used some form of puppetry to represent their Gods and legends.

Because puppeteers were itinerant nomadic people their stories and traditions travelled from land to land. In the middle ages the art became more prevalent in Europe and one of the most famous examples is the Commedia del'Arte in Italy in the 15th Century. Possibly the most widely known puppet show in the British Isles, Punch and Judy, originated in Italy as Pulcinella. A moral tale, its stories are still faithfully acted out today, often with references to current life.

For many years during the rule of Oliver Cromwell, the influence of Puritanism closed down many British theatres. Puppetry kept the art alive – as it was performed by street entertainers and fairground folk it was difficult to supress and would often have contained some satirical references to contemporary society.

Puppetry today

Puppets have always had the capability of expressing subtle human emotions. Although they are usually made from simple, everyday materials they seem to come alive when operated and draw the audience into a rich world of imagination. They can often reduce the most sophisticated of people to tears of laughter! Puppetry is still very much alive in our culture in its traditional form, passed on from generation to generation, and, in a contemporary form, very often used in television and in animated film.

Most people will have had at some stage in their life an opportunity to make a puppet, most probably a clumsy attempt at school. Puppets made by children often have a charming and endearing naive quality that adults find impossible to reveal in their own work – they often seem to be more concerned with the technique and forget that they are trying to portray a character.

Before beginning to make puppets yourself it is always worth looking at historic examples of the craft. Many examples exist in museums and theatrical collections, and viewing can be most inspiring and helpful. You will be adding your ideas and inventions to a long historical tradition.

The Projects

· · ·

This book consists of 13 exciting puppet projects which are inspired by traditional culture and the world of folk traditions, but which interpret the techniques, making them simple and accessible for all.

Puppet Types

There are basically four main types of puppet. Most of the projects in this book fit into these traditional categories, but there should be no doctrinaire rules about how to make them.

1. Stick Puppets

These are the most simple kinds of puppet. They generally don't actually move themselves but are held by a stick or handle which can be moved to make simple upward and downward or sideways gestures. Examples of stick puppets in this book are the wonderfully simple wooden spoon puppets, the birds on sticks, the cardboard cat mask. The inventive variation, the dancing skeleton, is operated with a stick from behind while the arms, legs and head bounce around independently as they are attached to the body with springs.

2. Glove Puppets

These are usually soft-bodied puppets which are operated by inserting the hand into the body, the small finger and the thumb operating the arms. This kind of puppet can be very simple, the five-fingered glove puppet and the felt finger puppets being the most easy examples to make. A more traditional puppet of this kind is the Crown Prince – its head is made of papier mâché and a sewn body and legs are stuffed and attached to the front of the tunic. The Marmalade Cat project is an example of the most common form of glove puppet. The Sock Dragon is very effective in that the whole hand and forearm fits into the sock and brings the dragon to life when it is manipulated.

A more unusual and topical variety of the traditional glove puppet is the Supermarket Shocker – the plastic bottle using discarded domestic materials to make a haunting alien masklike puppet which is operated by putting a hand into the bottle from behind.

4. Shadow Puppets

These are usually flat silhouettes of card, the arms or legs being jointed and moved with thin rods. The figure is held upright with another thin stick and operated against a translucent screen. A light is shone from behind the puppet and there should be some degree of darkness in front of the screen for dramatic effect. The Indian on a horse is a good example of a shadow puppet but can of course be operated without light and screen to good effect.

The Jumping Jack doesn't strictly fit into any of these four categories. Perhaps more of a mechanical toy, it has most in common with the shadow puppets, and it could be used as such if a stick was attached to it for holding.

3. String Puppets

There is strictly only one puppet in the book which fits into this category – The Acrobat. The figure is jointed at neck, elbows, waist and knees. The limbs and head are attached with strings to a wooden cross held horizontally above the puppet. By tilting the cross, you can make the puppet move most realistically – walking, jumping, dancing, or turning the head. This is the most sophisticated technique in puppet making, but the Acrobat in this book is much simplified and needs only careful attention and patience to produce a very effective example of this method.

A NOTE ON PAPIER MÂCHÉ PULP

- All the materials that are listed for each project are inexpensive and readily available. Proprietory pulp is available from craft or good toy shops. You may like to try making your own using the following method.
- Tear a newspaper into small squares, approximately 2 × 2cm/¾ × ¾in and put it all in a large saucepan. Cover with water and boil until the paper begins to disintegrate. Turn off the heat and allow to cool. Then mash with a potato masher, strain off the excess water, and squeeze the rest out with your hands.
- Add ½ cup of P.V.A adhesive, a sprinkling of dry cellulose or starch paste, ½ cup of proprietory wall filler and 1 cup of fine sawdust. Knead this mixture as you would bread, on a flat surface, until all the ingredients are well mixed. This mixture will keep for a number of weeks in the fridge.
- The projects on the following pages provide simple, clear instructions for making the puppets. They are really easy to follow and require no specialist equipment or knowledge – all can be made on the kitchen table.
- As you make these projects, new and original ideas will occur to you – try them out, invent your own characters, and keep alive one of the most enduring forms of international theatre!

Jumping Jack

This traditional puppet is seen in many cultures and something like it was perhaps the first moving toy to be made. We have made a simple version — with a feather in its cap — but the same principle can be used to make quite complicated puppets with many moving parts.

You will need
◊ Tracing paper
◊ Pencil
◊ Thin, ivory-coloured card
◊ Scissors
◊ Felt-tipped pens (yellow, black, orange and pink)
◊ Hole punch
◊ 5 paper fasteners
◊ Strong, black thread
◊ Feather
◊ Clear, all-purpose adhesive
◊ Small, wooden or glass bead

1 Transfer the template images to the card and carefully cut out the arms, legs and body.

Jumping Jack Templates

2 Colour the hair, hat band, lower legs and soles of the shoes yellow.

3 Colour the jacket and hat in pink and orange, using the illustration of the finished puppet for reference.

4 Colour the black areas of the boots and the striped breeches.

5 Pierce the holes shown on the template – one each at the shoulders and hips and two at the top of both arms and both legs.

6 Attach the arms and the legs to the body with paper fasteners, making sure that the limbs move freely before you turn back the tabs on the fasteners.

7 Thread the black thread through the other holes in the arms and the legs.

8 Stick a small, brightly coloured feather to the hat and secure it with the last paper fastener.

9 Fasten a small bead to the end of the thread.

Indian Warrior

This plucky Indian, inspired by American folk art weather-vanes, is easy to make and even easier to operate. You can use the same method to create more characters so that you can act out a complete drama.

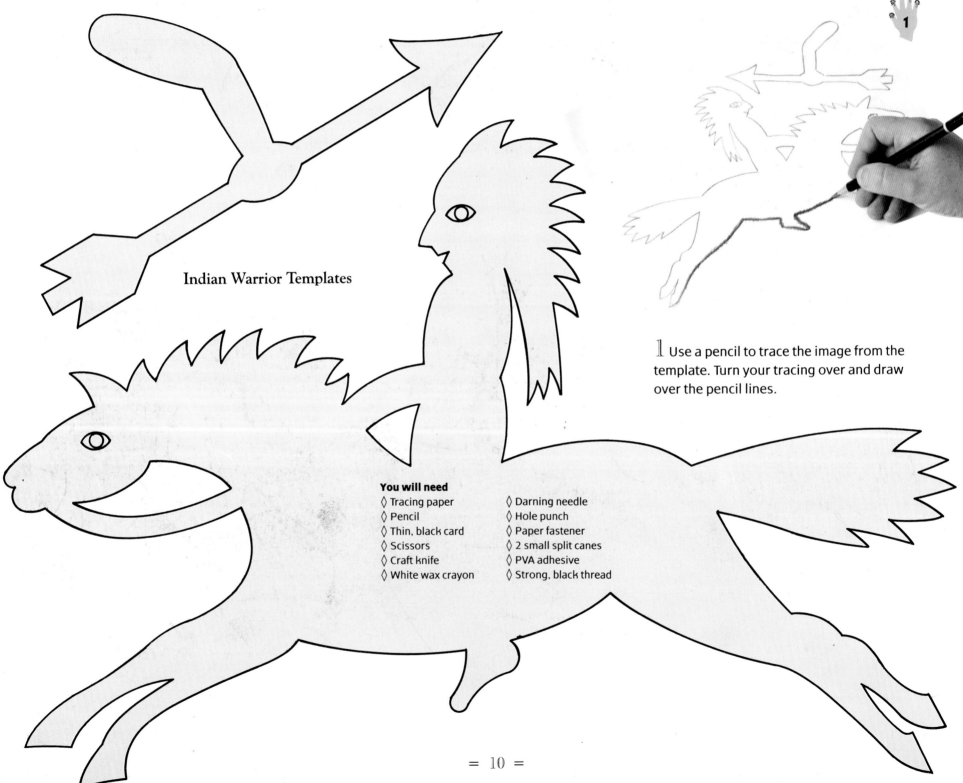

Indian Warrior Templates

You will need
- ◊ Tracing paper
- ◊ Pencil
- ◊ Thin, black card
- ◊ Scissors
- ◊ Craft knife
- ◊ White wax crayon
- ◊ Darning needle
- ◊ Hole punch
- ◊ Paper fastener
- ◊ 2 small split canes
- ◊ PVA adhesive
- ◊ Strong, black thread

1 Use a pencil to trace the image from the template. Turn your tracing over and draw over the pencil lines.

2 Turn over the tracing paper again and carefully draw over the original traced lines with a sharp pencil to transfer the image to the black card. Remove the tracing paper.

3 Accurately cut out the image.

4 Use a craft knife to cut out the parts that are not accessible with scissors – under the arms, for example.

5 Cut out the eyes with the point of your craft knife.

6 Highlight the image with a sharp white crayon. Don't forget to add the detail to the arm and arrow.

7 Use a darning needle to pierce a hole through the elbow of the arm carrying the arrow.

8 Position the arrow-carrying arm behind the body and pierce a hole through the two thicknesses at the "shoulder".

9 Push a paper fastener through the holes, making sure that the arm can be moved before you open out the tabs on the back.

10 Glue one piece of split cane to the centre of the back of the horse.

11 Make a small hole in the top of the other piece of cane and tie it loosely to the elbow with strong black thread.

Dragon

Don't throw away your old or odd socks. You can turn them into a host of colourful characters – monsters, a dragon like this one or whatever takes your imagination – and watch them metamorphose into a new existence.

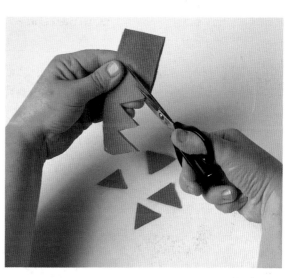

You will need
◊ Sewing thread
◊ 2 old socks
◊ Pins
◊ Scissors
◊ Needle
◊ Felt (orange, black, yellow and pink)
◊ Polyester stuffing
◊ Scrap material (for eyes)
◊ Fabric glue
◊ Sequins

1 Cut a slit down the back of one sock and a little way along the sole.

2 Cut a slit in the same sock on the upper foot and opposite the heel.

3 Cut off the toe of the other sock.

4 With right sides together, pin the toe section into the slit in the first sock.

5 Stitch the toe section in place to make the lower jaw.

6 Cut out a zigzag from the orange felt. It should be approximately 30cm/12in long.

7 Still with the sock inside out, place the zigzag along the slit up the back, pinning it so that the straight edge of the zigzag lies along the slit and the points lie inwards.

8 Use running stitch to stitch the zigzag in place.

9 Pull the sock through to the right side, to reveal the fins running down the back.

10 Stitch a neat line of small running stitches around the edge of a circle of pink fabric; do not fasten off the thread. Place a small wad of polyester stuffing in the centre.

11 Pull up the running stitches to form a ball and oversew to hold.

12 Sew the eyeballs onto the sock head, just in front of the end of the fins.

13 Use fabric glue to stick white sequins onto small circles of black felt. Stick the "eyes" onto the eyeballs.

14 Stitch on scraps of orange, yellow and pink felt as whiskers and glue sequins onto the ends at the points they are sewn to the head.

15 Cut out a forked tongue from yellow felt and sew it inside the mouth. Slide your arm into the sock, putting your thumb into the lower jaw.

Crafty Cat

This is one of the easiest stick puppets you can make — it's simply a cardboard shape on a stick. We have used the idea of a mask, a shape cut out from cardboard and then painted to create a striking image.

You will need
◊ Thin cardboard (from a cardboard box, for example)
◊ Felt-tipped pen (black)
◊ Scissors
◊ Craft knife
◊ Acrylic primer (white)
◊ Paintbrush
◊ Acrylic paint (green, white, blue, orange and yellow)
◊ All-purpose adhesive
◊ Flat stick

1 Draw a cat's head on cardboard with a black felt-tipped pen and cut around the outline with scissors.

2 Use a craft knife to cut out the slits for the eyes and mouth.

3 Paint a coat of acrylic primer over the whole face.

4 When the primer is dry, paint the face bright green.

5 Paint the nose in blue, adding white highlights.

6 Outline the eyes and mouth in blue, then paint white circles on either side of the nose for cheeks.

7

8

9

7 Paint some yellow shading on the cheeks to give a three-dimensional effect and add some orange dots.

8 Paint white inner ears, add yellow and orange stripes under the eyes and add a chin. Finally, edge the entire mask with blue.

9 Glue the stick firmly in place on the back of the mask.

Mr and Mrs Witherspoon

Wooden spoons are inexpensive and available in a variety of shapes and sizes. They always seem to impart a slightly prim feeling to the puppet faces. Use the method described here to make a whole cast of characters, or an entire family.

You will need
◊ White cartridge paper or lightweight card
◊ Felt-tipped pens (black, pink and blue)
◊ Scissors
◊ 1 wooden spoon
◊ Clear, all-purpose adhesive
◊ Stage hair (we used ginger)
◊ Sequins
◊ Ribbon

1 Use a black felt-tipped pen to draw two eyes on the white paper. Carefully cut out the eyes with scissors.

2 Glue the eyes to the wooden spoon, about one-third of the way from the top. Draw in the eyebrows and nose with black felt-tipped pen.

3 Use a pink felt-tipped pen to add the cheeks.

4 Draw in the mouth with pink felt-tipped pen and add a black line. Finish off the face with some blue eye-shadow.

5 Smear some adhesive along the top edge of the spoon.

6 Stick on the stage hair.

7 Stick a large green sequin on either side of the face, partly on the spoon and partly on the hair.

8 Tie the ribbon in a neat bow around the neck of the puppet and trim to length.

Dancing
Skeleton

• • •

This little puppet was inspired by the Day of the Dead Festival, when Mexicans eat sweets shaped like skulls. It's a simple puppet to make, but it dances in a macabre yet entertaining way. Use a proprietary papier mâché pulp if you do not want to make your own.

You will need
◊ Papier mâché pulp
◊ Knife
◊ 1 piece of 6mm/¼in dowel, 30cm/12in long
◊ 2 springs, each 13cm/5in long
◊ 2 springs, each 9cm/3½in long
◊ 1 spring, 3cm/1½in long
◊ Acrylic primer (white)
◊ Paintbrushes (medium and small)
◊ Acrylic paint (grey)

1 Model the body of the skeleton from papier mâché pulp with your hands, narrowing the waist and pinching out the pelvis.

2 Roll out small sausages of pulp and arrange them to form the ribs on the upper body.

3 Use a kitchen knife to model the vertebrae.

4 Push the pieces of dowel into the back of the skeleton's body to a depth of about 1cm/½in.

5 Use pulp to model a skull, making sure it is in proportion with the body. Use the end of the dowel to create eye sockets.

6 Use a knife to draw in the jaw and to make indentations to represent the teeth.

7 Press small amounts of pulp onto the ends of the four long springs to form the hands and feet. Insert the small spring into the base of the skull.

8 Insert the two longer springs into the hip bones and the two shorter springs at the shoulders of the skeleton body. The springs should go into the body to a depth of about 1cm/½in. Pack the springs with pulp, so that they are firmly embedded in the pulp.

9 Push the head spring into the top of the skeleton and pack it with more pulp to hold it firm. As the pulp dries out it will help to hold the springs in place. Leave the skeleton to dry in a warm place – an airing cupboard or an oven on a very low setting, for example.

10 When the skeleton is completely dry give the body, skull, hands and feet a coat of white primer. Take care that you do not get paint on the springs.

11 Leave the primer to dry then paint the outlines of the rib bones, eye sockets, jaw, teeth and pelvis in grey paint.

12 Paint in the outlines of the bones in the hands and feet in the same way.

13 Push the dowel into the hole in the back. If you wish you can use a spot of glue to hold it, but you may prefer to leave it so that you can take it out.

Flight of Fancy

Have you ever wondered what you can do with all the corks that you find left over after a party? Well, here's one answer — make a flock of birds. This is possibly the easiest of all the projects in the book and one that might lead you to your own flights of fancy. Try adding real feathers or sequins or use glittery paper.

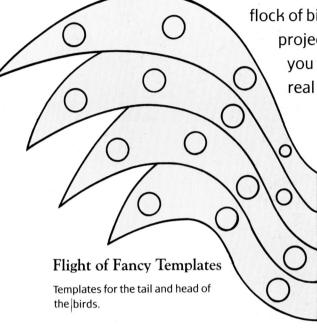

Flight of Fancy Templates

Templates for the tail and head of the birds.

You will need
◊ Tracing paper
◊ Pencil
◊ Thin white card
◊ Felt-tipped pens (yellow, orange, pink, blue, red and black)
◊ Scissors
◊ Craft knife
◊ Cork
◊ 1 piece of 6mm/¼in dowel, approximately 35cm/14in long

1 Transfer the outlines of the template to the white card, then, using the illustration of the finished puppet as a guide, begin to colour in the bird's head and tail with yellow and orange.

2 Use red for the crest and comb and blue to colour the face. Outline the beak and eyes with black.

3 Carefully add the pink spots to the tail.

4 When you have finished colouring, neatly cut out the head and tail.

5 Use a craft knife to cut a slit, about 6mm/¼in deep, across each end of the cork.

6 Use the point of a pair of closed scissors to make a hole in the bottom of the cork.

7 Insert the dowel into the hole in the cork.

8 Holding the dowel, colour the side of the cork blue and the ends pink.

9 Push the head and tail sections into the slits you have cut in the ends of the cork.

Marmalade Cat

• • •

This puppet is made using the
simple papier mâché layering technique. Instead
of decorating with paint, the cat's face is created using torn scrap paper. In
this way the construction and decoration of the puppet are part of the same
process.

Tunic Template.

Use this template to cut out
two pieces of material for the tunic.

You will need

◊ Plasticine (blue and yellow)
◊ Petroleum jelly
◊ Sugar paper (blue and orange; small
  amounts of yellow and green)
◊ Colourful wrapping paper (scraps of)
◊ Paste (cellulose or starch)
◊ Craft knife
◊ PVA adhesive
◊ Masking tape
◊ Cardboard tube
◊ Tracing paper

◊ Pencil
◊ Scissors
◊ Pins
◊ Scrap material, approximately 30 ×
  30cm/12 × 12in square × 2
◊ Pins
◊ Needle
◊ Sewing thread
◊ Orange felt, approximately 30 × 30cm/
  12 × 12in square × 2
◊ Orange embroidery thread

Cut out four mitten
pieces using this
template.

Mitten Template

1 Model the blue plasticine into a cat's head shape.

2 Using the yellow plasticine, make the features – the nose, eyebrows and two balls for the cheeks.

3 Make a collar out of yellow plasticine and add blue bobbles.

4 Smear the whole of the cat's head with an even coat of petroleum jelly to stop the paper from sticking to the plasticine.

5 Tear some of the orange sugar paper into small pieces and smear with paste, taking care not to make them too wet. Begin to cover the head with the paper, overlapping each piece.

6 When you have completely covered the head with orange paper, repeat the process with blue paper. Continue in this way, alternating the orange and blue, until you have applied seven layers. You should end with an orange layer.

7 Leave to dry thoroughly. This may take some time, but you can speed things up by putting the head in a warm place — an airing cupboard. for example. When it is dry use a craft knife to cut cleanly all around the head. Make sure that the blade cuts through the paper and into the plasticine beneath.

8 Prise the two halves of the head away from the plasticine — they should come away quite easily.

9 Put some PVA adhesive on the rim of one of the halves.

10 Carefully match the two halves together and hold them in place with small pieces of masking tape until the adhesive dries, which should take about 30 minutes.

11 When the adhesive is dry remove the masking tape and disguise the join by pasting small pieces of torn orange paper over it so that they blend in with the rest of the head.

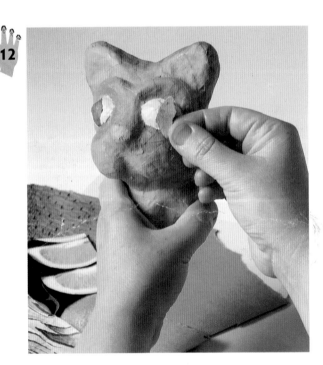

13 Stick some torn pieces of patterned orange paper onto the head. Cover the eyebrows and nose with blue paper and make a small mouth. Cover the collar with blue sugar paper and the raised bobbles with alternate yellow and orange scraps of wrapping paper.

12 Tear some yellow paper, and paste it onto the eyeballs. Use some green paper to make the pupils of the eyes.

14 Trace the tunic template, cut it out and pin it to a double thickness of material.

15 Carefully cut out the tunic.

16 Trace the hand templates, cut them out and pin each of them to two pieces of felt. Cut them out.

17 Make the hands by stitching the two layers of felt together with orange embroidery thread.

18 With the tunic still the wrong way out, turn up the hem and stitch the side, underarm and shoulder seams together, leaving spaces at the neck and cuffs.

19 Turn the tunic the right way round.

20 Turn down the edge of the cuff to the inside, slot in the hand and neatly stitch it in place. Repeat with the other hand.

21 Push a small section of cardboard tube into the neck of the tunic and stick it in place with PVA adhesive.

22 Apply some adhesive to the inside of the cat's head around the collar.

23 Push the head onto the cardboard tube, making sure that the collar covers the join with the tunic. Hold it in place until the adhesive is dry.

Crown Prince

This regal-looking character has rather humble origins — paper pulp and scrap material. Although it is a more elaborate puppet to make than some of the others, each stage is straightforward and requires no specialist technique or knowledge. The method is the one used to make traditional Punch-and-Judy-style puppets, and once you have mastered the approach you could easily go on to make all the characters in a fairy story.

You will need
◊ Newspaper
◊ Cardboard tube
◊ Masking tape
◊ Papier mâché pulp
◊ Knife
◊ Acrylic primer (white)
◊ Paintbrushes (small and medium)
◊ Acrylic paints (blue, pink, red, yellow, brown and black)
◊ Plate or palette for mixing paints
◊ Gold paper or gold foil
◊ Scissors

◊ Clear, all-purpose adhesive
◊ Tracing paper
◊ Pencil
◊ Pins
◊ Gold-coloured velvet, 2 pieces, 35 × 40cm/14 × 17in
◊ Needle
◊ Sewing thread
◊ 4 rubber bands
◊ Polyester stuffing
◊ PVA adhesive
◊ Gold-coloured braid, 2m/6ft

Trouser Template

Trouser legs. Cut out four trouser pieces using this template.

For the Prince's tunic, use the template for the Marmalade Cat, on page 26. Cut out 2 pieces of material.

1 Scrunch up a ball of newspaper so that it is the size of your fist. Secure the newspaper ball to the top of a cardboard tube with masking tape.

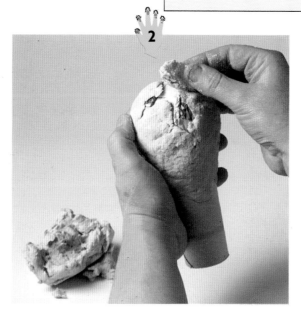

2 Evenly cover the newspaper with a layer of pulp. Use a proprietary mix if you don't want to make your own. Smooth down the pulp onto the tube, which will form the neck, and leave to dry overnight.

3 Begin to model the nose, pressing the pulp well onto the head and smoothing out any joins. Add the eyes and eyebrows.

4 Make the lips and add a moustache and some hair. Model the crown by simply making even points around the head. When you have finished, leave the head to dry thoroughly, ideally for several days.

5 Use some more pulp to model the boots.

6 Make a clearly defined dent all around the top of each boot with a knife. The dent will make it easier to attach the trouser legs later on. Leave to dry thoroughly.

7 Model the hands with pulp, remembering to make a separate thumb. Use a knife to make a dent around the wrists of both hands. Leave to dry.

8 When the boots are dry give them a coat of white acrylic primer. When the head is dry give it a coat of white acrylic primer.

9 Use the medium paintbrush to paint the crown blue.

10 Paint the hair pale yellow and the face a flesh tone. Make rosy cheeks by mixing red with the flesh colour on the face before it dries. Paint the lips bright red. Paint the eyes blue and the moustache and eyebrows dark brown. Add a dark brown line around the eyes.

11 Use a darker shade of yellow to add some rough streaks over the hair. When the paint is dry, add some dark brown lines.

12 Paint some fine, pale yellow lines on the moustache and eyebrows.

13 Paint the hands flesh pink.

14 Paint the boots blue, but paint the soles of the boots black.

15 Tear or cut out pieces of gold paper or foil and stick them to the points of the crown. Cut a long, narrow piece of foil to go around the base of the crown. Glue it in place.

16 Trace and cut out the templates for the tunic and trousers. Pin the templates onto two layers of the fabric, folded with right sides together.

17 Carefully cut out two legs and one tunic.

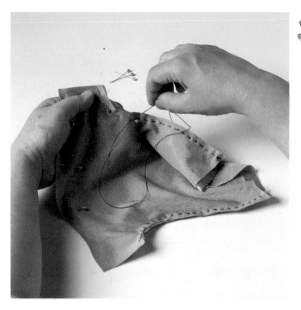

18 Use a neat running stitch to sew together the seams of the body and the trouser legs.

19 Remember not to sew up the cuffs or the top and bottom ends of the trouser legs.

20 Push a boot into a trouser leg so that the boot is completely covered by the trouser leg.

21 Wind a rubber band tightly around the boot where the dent is. Make sure the rubber band is as tight as possible.

22 Pull the trouser leg the right way round.

23 Put a little polyester filling in the leg, but do not fill it too full. Repeat for the other leg.

24 Push a hand, fingers first, into the cuff of the tunic, which is still inside out. Wind a rubber band tightly around the hand, making sure it rests in the ridge around the wrist. Make sure the rubber band is as tight as possible.

25 Repeat with the other hand, then pull the tunic the right way out to reveal the firmly attached hands.

26 Smear some PVA adhesive around the neck and push the tunic onto the neck, over the line of adhesive.

27 Pin, then stitch the legs to the front of the bottom of the tunic.

28 Stick gold braid around the neck, cuffs and down the front of the tunic.

29 Finally, stick braid around the hem of the tunic, covering the stitching that attaches the legs.

The Acrobat

— • • • —

At last — here are simple instructions for making an articulated string puppet. These are usually quite complicated, technical projects, but when you make this acrobat you make the joints at the same time you make the puppet, so all you need is patience. You can use a proprietary papier mâché pulp if you do not want to make your own.

You will need

- ◊ Thin galvanized wire
- ◊ Wire cutters
- ◊ Pliers
- ◊ Newspaper
- ◊ Wallpaper paste
- ◊ Papier mâché pulp
- ◊ Acrylic primer (white)
- ◊ Paintbrushes (medium and small)
- ◊ Acrylic paint (black, yellow, blue and red)
- ◊ Clear, all-purpose adhesive
- ◊ Stage hair

- ◊ Bradawl
- ◊ 2 lengths of wood, each 1.5 × 1.5 × 20cm/ ¾ × ¾ × 8in
- ◊ 1 length of wood, 1.5 × 1.5 × 30cm/¾ × ¾ × 12in
- ◊ Screw, approximately 2.5cm/1in long
- ◊ Screwdriver
- ◊ 7 eye hooks
- ◊ 2 lengths of strong thread, each approximately 50cm/20 in
- ◊ 2 lengths of strong thread, each approximately 40cm/16in
- ◊ 1 length of strong thread, approximately 30cm/12in

1 Cut a length of wire approximately 60cm/2ft long. Twist a loop in the middle of this — this will be the loop in the top of the puppet's head — and roughly wind the rest of the wire around itself to make a head shape. Leave a loop of wire at what will be the neck joint.

2 Thread a length of wire, a little longer than the first piece, through the loop at the bottom of the head and twist it to secure it; this will be the neck joint. Continue twisting and bending the wire to form the shape of the upper body. Make wire loops at the shoulders and waist.

3 Use lengths of wire, approximately 50cm/21in in length, to make a pelvis, the upper arms and the upper legs, attaching the limbs and body sections with loops of wire as before.

4 Add the lower arms and hands, using approximately 60cm/25in lengths of wire, leaving an upstanding loop of wire on each wrist, which are not articulated. These loops will be used to attach the arm strings.

5 Make the lower legs and feet in the same way, again using 60cm/25in lengths of wire. No loops are needed here because the leg strings are attached at the knees.

6 Tear a length of newspaper so that it is approximately 8cm/3in wide and smear it lightly on both sides with paste.

7 Start to wind the newspaper around all the sections of the puppet, making sure that you leave all the wire loop joins free. Use two layers to build up the shape of the body.

8 Begin to add paper pulp to the head and body, making sure that you add an even layer, about 6mm/¼in deep all over, although you can use more pulp to give the puppet more shape if necessary.

9 When you add pulp to the lower arm take care that you keep the wire loop at the wrist free.

10 Use extra pulp to model the features on the face. Put the puppet in a warm place – an airing cupboard or an oven on a very low setting, for example – and leave to dry thoroughly.

11 When it is dry, paint the whole puppet with one coat of acrylic primer. Use the small paintbrush to paint blue eyes, black pupils and eyebrows, and the nose and mouth. Paint on red spots for the cheeks.

12 Paint the puppet's upper legs, the arms as far as the wrists and the body as far as the neck yellow. Paint a red outline around the neck, wrists and lower legs, then paint red spots on the yellow costume.

13 Carefully paint black ballet shoes on the puppet's feet.

14 Smear some adhesive over the top of the head. Arrange some stage hair on the adhesive on the head and hold it in place until the adhesive is dry. Make sure the loop of wire at the top of the head is not covered with hair.

15 Use a bradawl to make a hole in the centre of the longer piece of wood and in the centre of one of the shorter pieces of wood.

16 Screw these two lengths of wood firmly together.

17 Using eye hooks to form a moving joint, attach the other length of wood. Attach the remaining eye hooks.

18 Attach lengths of strong thread to the loops at the knees (approximately 50cm/20in), at the wrists (approximately 40cm/16in) and at the top of the head (approximately 30cm/12in). Fasten the knots tightly.

19 Attach the other ends of the strings to the loops on the lengths of wood. The leg strings are joined to the moving section of wood; the arm strings are attached to the fixed section; and the head string is attached to the eye hook fixed just behind the crosspiece that holds the arm strings.

Supermarket Shocker

— ● ● ● —

Be more creative with your rubbish. You can make some extraordinary characters from the mass of throwaway packaging that finds its way into our rubbish bins every day. You might even find yourself looking along the supermarket shelves, looking out for interesting shapes that you can transform into extraterrestrial puppets.

You will need
◊ Large plastic bottle (we used a 2 litre/
   3½ pint milk bottle)
◊ Craft knife
◊ Paper or fabric dishcloth (we used J-cloths)
◊ Thin piece of wood with rounded end (we used a
   chopstick)

◊ Plastic squeezy lemon
◊ Scissors
◊ 2 bottle tops
◊ Small block of wood
◊ Hole punch
◊ 2 paper fasteners

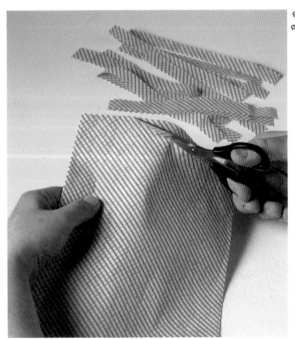

1 Using a craft knife, carefully cut away the back section (that is, opposite to the handle) of the plastic bottle.

2 Again using the craft knife, make a series of small slits around the top of what will be the head of your puppet.

3 Cut the paper dishcloth into strips, approximately 1cm/½in wide.

4 Fold a cut strip in two and push it into the slit with the rounded end of a thin piece of wood.

5 Cut off the screw-top from the plastic lemon.

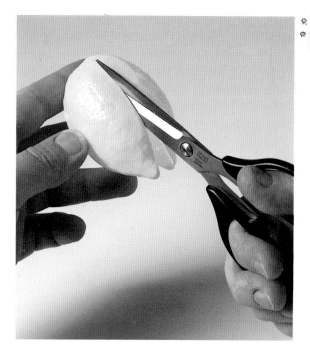

6 Cut the lemon in half lengthways; there is usually a joining line to follow.

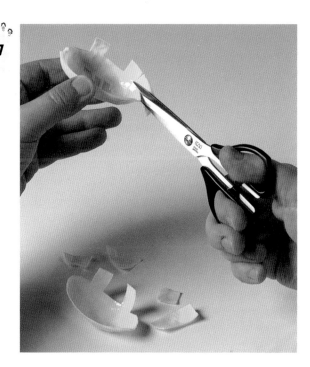

7 Cut each half of the lemon into ear shapes, leaving small tabs to fix them to the head. Remember to cut each shape differently to suit the right and left sides.

8 Cut slots in the sides of the bottle head to correspond with the ears, bearing in mind that the handle of the bottle will be the nose.

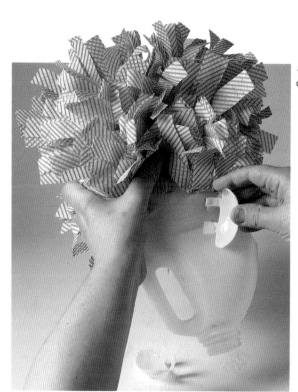

9 Push the ear tabs into the slots in the head.

10 Place a bottle top on the block of wood and pierce a hole through the centre with the hole punch.

11 Push a paper fastener through the hole in the bottle top.

12 Use the hole punch to make holes in the front of the face, one on each side of the handle.

13 Place a bottle top eye over the hole and hold it in place by pushing the tabs of the paper fastener through the hole and, with your hand inside the bottle, pressing open the tabs. Repeat with the other eye.

Felt Friends

These small finger puppets are an ideal way to use up odd bits of felt that you might have left over from some of the other projects. Make them as bright and jolly as you can. You could add sequins, beads, jewels or feathers to make them look more elaborate.

Cut out two pieces of felt using this template.

Felt Friends Templates

Cut out two pieces of felt using this template.

1 Trace and cut out the templates. Pin the body template to the green felt. Cut out two pieces.

2 Cut out one pink hair shape and one red hair shape.

3 Cut the longer sides of the red and pink felt shapes into a fringe.

4 Stick sequins to the front of one of the green felt body pieces to make eyes, using a large sequin underneath and a smaller one on top for the pupil.

5 Cut small strips of orange felt and stick them to the face as eyebrows and a nose.

You will need
◊ Tracing paper
◊ Pencil
◊ Pins
◊ Felt (green, pink, red, orange)
◊ Sequins
◊ Fabric glue

6 Glue the red cheeks in place.

7 Position the pink hair on the inside of the back body piece. Glue it down.

8 Stick the red hair directly on top of the pink hair.

9 Stick the green body piece with the face on it to the back body piece so that the red and pink hair pieces are sandwiched between, with just the fringe showing.

Finger Family

What could be simpler than to convert an old glove into a family of whimsical characters? Each one has its own expression and entertaining hairstyle. You might want to have a happy family on one hand and a miserable family on the other.

You will need
◊ 1 woollen glove (we used an orange glove)
◊ White sequins
◊ Small, black beads
◊ Needle
◊ Sewing thread
◊ 1 piece of 1.5cm/¾in wooden dowel, approximately 30cm/12in long
◊ Darning needle
◊ Tapestry wool (black, yellow, orange, green, pink and blue)
◊ Scissors

1 Put the glove on and sew white sequins and black beads onto each finger as eyes.

2 Push the piece of dowel into each finger in turn to support it while you sew.

3 Use black tapestry wool to sew eyebrows and the line of a nose on each face. Stitch the nose straight down between the sequin eyes.

4 Sew on the mouth with yellow wool, changing the expression on each finger.

5 Using a different colour for each finger, sew loops of tapestry wool to make the hair.

6 Trim the loops of hair evenly around each face.